IMAGES
of America

BELCHERTOWN
STATE SCHOOL

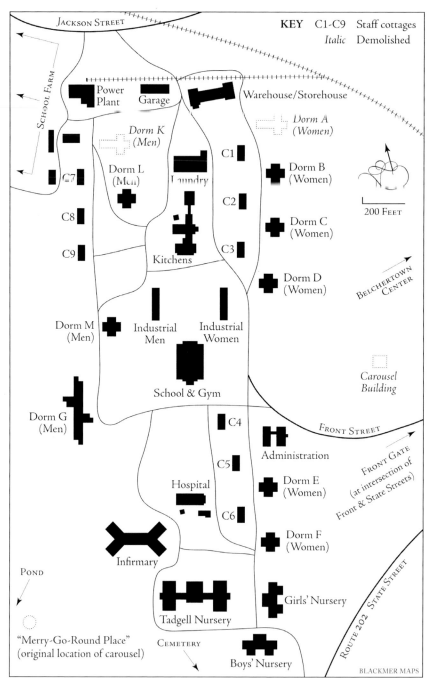

This map of the Belchertown State School campus was created by Kate Blackmer of Blackmer Maps for Robert Hornick's book *The Girls and Boys of Belchertown*. It can also be found in Ed Orzechowsi's *You'll Like It Here*. (Courtesy of Kate Blackmer and Robert Hornick.)

ON THE COVER: Pictured on the cover is an early classroom in the schoolhouse, completed in 1928 and expanded to add more classroom space in 1932. (Courtesy of the Don LaBrecque Collection at the Department of Developmental Services.)

IMAGES
of America

BELCHERTOWN
STATE SCHOOL

Katherine Anderson
Foreword by Robert N. Hornick

ARCADIA
PUBLISHING

Published by Arcadia Publishing
Charleston, South Carolina

Printed in the United States of America

Library of Congress Control Number: 2019957409

For all general information, please contact Arcadia Publishing:
Telephone 843-853-2070
Fax 843-853-0044
E-mail sales@arcadiapublishing.com
For customer service and orders:
Toll-Free 1-888-313-2665

Visit us on the Internet at www.arcadiapublishing.com

*This book is dedicated, as always, to my parents
and my husband, Bruce—my greatest fans.*

CONTENTS

FOREWORD

The college I attended in the 1960s was not far from Belchertown, but I had never heard of Belchertown State School until, in my sophomore or junior year, a classmate invited me to join him doing some volunteer work at the school. An acquaintance of his who worked there in administration was recruiting students for various projects, including weekly outdoor play, which my friend and I would oversee for a couple of semesters. Our charges were boys from one of the residential cottages, so-called "higher-functioning types"; however, their abilities were not uniform. Several also had physical disabilities. We would arrive in early afternoon, enter the noise-filled cottage, help our group put on jackets and coats, and then run with them outside to a nearby playing field where my classmate would organize various games. I looked after the quiet ones.

My clearest memory is of a young boy who liked to go for walks. He was remarkably articulate and sensitive. I vividly remember standing with him one brisk autumn afternoon on a path above the lake, listening to him describe, with feeling and nuance, the beauty of the woods around us. I couldn't understand why he was at Belchertown State School. Sadly, my curiosity was not sufficiently aroused at the time to pursue it. Only many years later did I come to understand that some kids were committed because parents couldn't or wouldn't take care of them due to delinquency, hyperactivity, attention deficit disorder, or another disability not involving intelligence. My young friend should not have been there in the first place. I long ago forgot his name but have been haunted over the years by my memory of him.

I did not know then about the dreadful conditions at the infirmary or the infamous A and K Wards or, more broadly, the "Tragedy of Belchertown" that would be sensationally exposed in a series of newspaper articles a few years later. I would eventually learn much more about these, and other indignities, after I retired from law practice and began to write a book about the social history of the state school. By that time, the school was permanently closed, the premises were abandoned, and the last residents of the place had either been moved to other institutions or transferred into community living alternatives in the western part of the state. I spent many hours over a period of several years doing research at the Clapp Memorial Library in Belchertown, the Belchertown Historical Association, the libraries of nearby colleges and towns, and the public and state libraries in Boston reading, among other things, old newspapers, annual reports, investigative reports, memoirs, and the like. I met many men and women who had had connections to the school—former residents who were compelled to live there, the relatives and friends of former residents, former employees and volunteers, state officials with the Department of Developmental Services, and citizens of the town of Belchertown itself. I walked the abandoned school grounds a number of times and visited the school cemetery in a pine grove near the intersection of Routes 21 and 202, where some 200 former residents are buried. I tried to imagine the lives lived and lost in these surroundings.

In the course of my research and writing, I came to believe that the history of Belchertown State School was more complicated than I had first thought. The tragedy was in many ways even more horrific than the newspaper exposé had portrayed, but there were also reforms that were implemented following the exposé. There were, too, unremembered acts of kindness and love throughout the school's history that comprised an important part of the story.

During most of the 20th century, people we today call "intellectually disabled" (we used to call them "feebleminded," "mentally retarded," and other things), were often confined—involuntarily—in large, publicly funded institutions. These institutions were located in small towns and villages like Belchertown, removed from major population centers. At their peak in the 1960s, they housed more than 190,000 men, women, and children in the United States.

When Belchertown State School opened in 1922, it had a clear pedagogical as well as custodial purpose. Rather quickly, however, the teaching purpose was overtaken by the custodial. The pressure built quickly to commit more and more people there—especially after the Great Depression began in 1929. The school population grew rapidly, increasing from several hundred in the 1920s to more than 1,500 by 1940. Moreover, from the start, the state school did not have sufficient paid staff to attend to all of its internal needs. It required unpaid, resident labor to do a lot of the work. This created a further incentive to keep the more-able, hardworking residents at the school rather than release them. In sum, the school acquired a permanent, increasingly aging population.

It was also the case, particularly after the onset of the Depression, that the school admitted more and more severely physically disabled persons—thus changing to some extent the kinds of facilities, care, and teaching that were required. Meanwhile, state funding did not keep up with the population growth or the changing demographics of the institution—again, the Great Depression exacerbated this. Therefore, construction, maintenance, and paid staffing could not keep up with the school's needs. Thus, caring for and controlling—not teaching—a large, increasingly disabled, and aging, resident population became the chief mission of the state school. Tragedy was bound to follow, and it did.

Some reforms were eventually adopted. For example, buildings were repaired, additional attendants and teachers were hired, and volunteer programs were expanded. More consequential, new ideas about how to teach and care for the intellectually disabled began taking hold. The very idea of confining intellectually disabled persons in large state institutions was being challenged. Most of those who thought about it came to believe that the large institutions should be closed and that, instead, the disabled should be resettled in the community in what are generally called "group homes." The reason is simple but powerful. As Edward Moscovitch states in *Mental Retardation Programs: How Does Massachusetts Compare?*, "Like the rest of us, people with mental retardation enjoy a chance to walk along a neighborhood street, to buy their own food, clothing and sundries, to go into a restaurant for ice cream or a meal, to go to the park on Sunday afternoon. Most important, like the rest of us, they need what a family offers—stable, mutual, loving relationships with a small number of people who care about them and live with or near them." Less often remarked but no less important, the lives of the rest of us are enriched by their presence in our communities in the same way that we are enriched anytime we make the acquaintance of another human being who is not intent on harming us.

Belchertown State School closed in 1992. It needed to be closed. It is important, however, that we not forget the lives lived and lost there—fellow human beings who were quarantined on the pretext of catering to their special needs but who too often became victims of society's fear that intellectual disability was inheritable and that compulsory isolation was the only way to avoid contamination.

This retelling of the state school's history through long-forgotten photographs brings that history to life in a way that words alone cannot. It is a welcome addition to the literature about Belchertown State School and will help us to remember what we must not forget.

—Robert Hornick
Author of *The Girls and Boys of Belchertown:
A Social History of the Belchertown State School for the Feeble-Minded*
(University of Massachusetts Press, 2012)

ACKNOWLEDGMENTS

First and foremost, this book is dedicated to the memory of Donald LaBrecque, a former trainer at the Massachusetts Department of Developmental Services who worked tirelessly to preserve and share the history of the treatment of individuals with disabilities including images, records, oral histories, and video recordings. Without him, much of this history would be lost.

Unless otherwise noted, all images in this book appear courtesy of the Don LaBrecque Collection at the Department of Developmental Services.

Don's incredible collection is now held by Laurie Whitney and Kathy Ekmalian at DDS. Laurie and Kathy welcomed me into their space and allowed me to immerse myself in nearly a century of memories for the better part of a year. As well, Cliff McCarthy of the Stone House Museum in Belchertown contributed a number of images from the museum's collection, and a good deal of research material was provided by the Clapp Memorial Library.

This book also owes a great deal to a number of others who have, along the way, become part of the state school historical canon: Jeromie Whalen, Steven Kaplan, Ed Orzechowski, and Robert N. Hornick, who provided the foreword for this volume.

No book about the state school would be possible without those who have a passion for history and preservation. Thanks go to Jill Bierly, Courtney Keating, Jen Turner, April Jasak-Bangs, Sarah Maroney, and all the members of the Belchertown Cultural Alliance and Belchertown State School Friends Association, all of whom enthusiastically took up the fight to bring the state school's legacy into the future.

And finally, to the former staff, residents, and their families—especially Kathy Post, Pat Vitkus, and Richard Dresser—whose support means more than they know—thank you for sharing this history with all of us.

The author's proceeds from the sale of this book will go to the Belchertown State School Friends Association.

INTRODUCTION

It has been more than a decade since the first time I visited the abandoned Belchertown State School in 2003. It was the first snow of the season, and the buildings were sealed tight, the campus completely silent except for the sound of falling snow. For more than 75 years, the state school occupied nearly 900 acres of what was once a group of family farms straddling Route 202 near the center of Belchertown, and though there wasn't much to see on that first visit, it wasn't long before an inexplicable wave of vandalism left the buildings open, giving me the opportunity to photograph them.

At the time, I was working at a residential treatment facility in Western Massachusetts and found that quite a few of my coworkers had started their careers at Belchertown, some in the 1970s at the height of the state school's greatest difficulties. After having read a number of accounts of the state school and the lawsuit that eventually closed it, I expected these people to be bitter, perhaps to speak ill of the school. Instead, they shared memories of taking residents home for the holidays, of buying them gifts, and helping to plan dances and special events. Despite circumstances not of their making, these people had done their best to make the residents' lives as normal and happy as they possibly could, and I knew there had to be more stories like that.

I started writing my first book on institutions in 2006 when we initially heard about potential redevelopment at the state school. The campus was going to be transformed into an upscale resort and spa, and the developer promised to retain as many of the original buildings as possible. While the Quabbin Resort Development was eventually scrapped and the property returned to the town, I was determined to see some part of the campus preserved. Development stalled, and the campus continued to sit, vacant and untouched, until 2015, when demolition began. The town partnered with MassDevelopment to begin clearing parcels, making way for Christopher Heights, a new senior living complex being built on the site of the old hospital.

Preserving the legacy of the state school—both the positive and the negative—has become a priority for me. In 2019, I, along with a newly appointed board, revived the Belchertown State School Friends Association with the intention of saving and reusing the Administration Building. Regardless of the outcome of that proposal, the friends intend to be the keepers of the history of all state schools in Massachusetts, making it all available to the public so that everyone has the opportunity to learn from the past.

The following is a note on terms: as this is a historical record, many of the terms used in this book are of the time period. While they may be considered offensive today, they were considered scientifically correct at the time that the state schools were operating and therefore appear in this book. In the early 1900s, the classifications of moron, idiot, and imbecile were added to the standard IQ test in order to group children with lower than average IQs. As well, individuals with cognitive disabilities were referred to as feebleminded or mentally defective. These terms are no longer used, and IQ testing is no longer employed as the sole method of determining intelligence. Further, attitudes about intelligence have changed substantially since the era of institutionalization.

Whereas many practitioners believed that intelligence was a fixed entity, which led to lifelong commitment for many with low IQs , we are now well aware that intelligence is fluid and can be influenced by a great many factors.

There are also some terms in this book that require a bit of explanation. In the early years, there were both custodial and noncustodial dorms on the state school campus. Custodial meant long-term or lifelong commitment, whereas noncustodial cases were short-term stays. Later, residents were further separated based on whether they were ambulatory   could get around on their own—or nonambulatory, which meant either bedridden or wheelchair bound. And finally, the terms used to describe those committed to state schools are numerous. At various times, they were referred to as students, inmates, residents, tenants, patients, and clients. These terms are used interchangeably throughout this book depending on the source of the information and the time period in which it was initially recorded.

The state school system was created with the best of intentions, but it was, after all, a human enterprise. When we are charged with caring for the most vulnerable of our society, we often find ourselves in the difficult position of operating within the rigid confines of an unforgiving bureaucracy. Out of the ashes of these institutions rose a new understanding of cognitive, developmental, and physical disabilities.

One

MOVING WEST

In January 1846, a state commission led by Samuel Gridley Howe conducted an inquiry into the status of feebleminded children in Massachusetts. Howe found that most were secluded in their homes as it was said that they could not be educated—Howe believed otherwise. He presented his findings, and on October 10, 1848, he was granted permission to open the first public school in the United States for feebleminded children. (Courtesy of Massachusetts Historical Association.)

The first school, with a classroom of 10 children, operated out of a disused wing of the Perkins Institute for the Blind, of which Howe was director. Within the first year, it was clear the children were progressing and their health and overall hygiene habits were improving remarkably, as well as their basic kindergarten skills. When the Joint Committee on Public Charitable Institutions visited in March 1851, they were so impressed by Howe's success with the feebleminded children that the school was given a more permanent location in South Boston. This was, however, a double-edged sword. Many parents and educators presumed that, given the school's success, the children would simply remain in the institution for life. Instead, Howe was adamant that his students were learning these skills for one reason only—to return to their homes and to their home schools where they could be with their typically developing peers, rather than isolated in a separate school. (Courtesy of Perkins School for the Blind Archives, Watertown, Massachusetts.)

The school remained in South Boston from 1856 until the student body had expanded to the point that a larger campus became necessary. The new property was a 180-acre parcel purchased by the state in 1887. Located in the Boston suburb of Waltham, the parcel was near the Waverley station of the Fitchburg & Massachusetts Central Railroad, and so, the Massachusetts School for the Feeble-Minded was referred to as "Waverley" in order to differentiate it from the South Boston location. Howe supervised the move to Waverley, and the school was officially opened on March 6, 1890; however, the move from South Boston would not be complete until December 1891. Under the direction of its first superintendent, Walter E. Fernald, the school flourished, and the student body expanded as routines of classroom education, industrial training, and recreational activities were established. (Author's collection.)

School Building & Recreation Rooms
Wrentham State School.

By the turn of the 20th century, the Massachusetts School for the Feeble-Minded had reached its peak population, well over 1,000 students, and the state approved the construction of a second school, preferably in a suburb south of Boston where a number of the Waverley students had been admitted from. The trustees of the Massachusetts school purchased a 450-acre campus in Wrentham, and the second state school opened on April 1, 1910. The first wave of patients admitted were transferred from Waltham, followed by more than 200 admissions from the surrounding community. The Waverley campus served as a parent institution while Wrentham quickly established itself as a leader in the training of feebleminded youth. Once the population at Wrentham began to climb, the trustees recommended that a third school be constructed in the western part of Massachusetts to serve the ever-growing number of admissions from that region. (Courtesy of Museum of disABILITY History.)

In 1915, the Massachusetts legislature announced that a $50,000 appropriation had been set aside to construct the third school for the feebleminded, sparking fierce competition among a number of Western Massachusetts towns, including Westfield, Conway, and Belchertown. The town of Belchertown lobbied hard, led by the newly formed board of trade established in 1914 with the sole purpose of expanding Belchertown's economy. The board was led by president and local entrepreneur Daniel Dwight Hazen, who became the strongest supporter of the new state school. He was so determined to have the state school located in Belchertown that he traveled by train to Boston to plead the town's case to the legislature, presumably in order to edge out the city of Holyoke (a last-minute entry). It was rumored that the town had already passed on the opportunity to be the home of Amherst College; this time, it was not going to miss out. (Courtesy of Belchertown Historical Association.)

Despite never having a chance to meet with the legislators, Hazen's trip to Boston was rewarded and Belchertown was chosen as the school's location. The entire town celebrated the victory. Once the decision was made in Belchertown's favor, the funds were released for the purchase of land for the state school. The acreage that was to be acquired for the state school would include land farmed by the Stacy, Michel, Howard, Witt, and Jepson families, who had been farming there for more than a century. Once the land was acquired, the Jepson farmhouse, shown here, along with the Howard and Michel farmhouses, were to be used to house the first staff and students sent from Wrentham, who would begin working the farm by 1916. During the initial phases of the state school's creation, Wrentham served as parent institution and would do so until the main campus was constructed six years later. (Courtesy of Belchertown Historical Association.)

Initially, there was a great deal of disappointment when the townspeople realized that the state school would be taking farmland away from some of the most prominent families in town. However, the first four parcels were acquired quite easily at what was considered a very fair price. The only hitch in the plan was David Jepson. He had inherited the farm from his father and had no desire to sell, and unfortunately, his property was the linchpin to the entire project. His acreage was bounded by the Central Vermont Railroad, which had agreed to build a spur track to the state school for free. The spur track would run right up to the storehouse, shown here in 1922 as it was nearing completion. The town elders eventually cornered Jepson at Colby's Barbershop and threatened him with eminent domain. He finally sold for $7,500 cash.

In April 1919, the Senate Ways and Means Committee approved the bill that released $150,000 for the construction of two dorms, service buildings, and campus infrastructure, but the project stalled almost immediately. Ironically, a viable water source, which had initially knocked the town of Conway out of the running, could not be located. The town was in the uncomfortable position of requesting an additional $50,000 to pipe water in from another location nearly two miles away. It was a massive and unexpected delay, making it impossible to lay the first foundations until the spring of 1921. (Both, courtesy of Stone House Museum.)

Despite the initial disappointing delays, the first ceremonial connection was made between the town and the school when state representative Roland D. Sawyer presented Belchertown's Clapp Memorial Library with the pen used by Gov. Samuel McCall, pictured here, to sign the resolve providing for the initial state school construction appropriation. In the meantime, the newly formed Commission on Mental Diseases, which replaced the State Board of Insanity in 1916, began the search for an architect to design the main campus. They chose the firm of Kendall, Taylor & Co. of Billerica who had designed the Wrentham campus as well as a number of other state institutions, including parts of Medfield State Hospital, Westborough State Hospital, Boston State Hospital, Monson State Hospital, Taunton State Hospital, Lyman School for Boys, and the Lancaster Reform School. (Author's collection.)

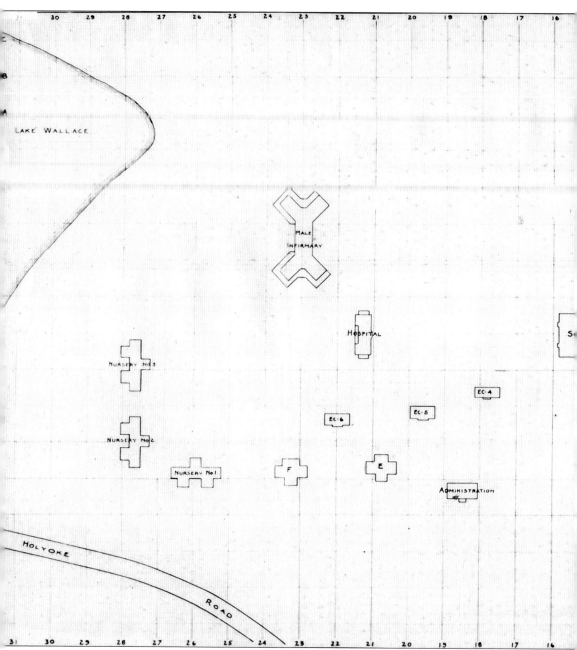

The state school campus was designed on the cottage plan—a collection of one- or two-story buildings, generally made of brick or other fireproof materials, laid out in the style of a college campus, nearly identical to that of Wrentham State School. Despite the fact that the campus was still an active construction site, it was declared "complete" enough for opening ceremonies on

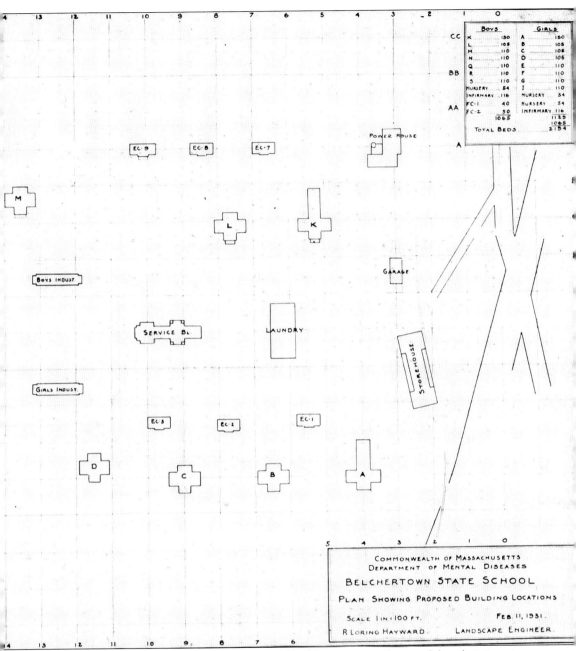

November 15, 1922. Only one third of the planned buildings were in place, and the administration offices were temporarily housed in the storehouse and bakery. The school opened with 197 male patients, 87 staff members, and 2 resident physicians.

Belchertown State School was often spoken of in reference to its similarity to a New England college campus, the buildings built solidly of redbrick and the grounds painstakingly landscaped behind carefully laid stone walls. By 1935, the state school was home to nearly 1,500 feebleminded children living on campus with the intention of expanding to accommodate 2,500 in the near future. In the November 17, 1922, edition of the *Belchertown Sentinel*, it was said, "Here then in our midst is an institution whose very existence is made possible by an advanced civilization. Here will be gathered through the years those who . . . ask for special opportunities . . . And here also will come those who have a sympathetic understanding of the needs of the unfortunate and will give their years in an effort to help them."

One dorm (Ward L) and one custodial building housed the first group of patients. Ward K, the custodial ward, was a large brick building shaped like an elongated cross and can be seen here. Pictures were hung on the walls, and cabinets in the common areas were filled with toys and games. The press was invited to tour the campus, and an early piece in the *Springfield Sunday Republican* described the boys singing in the day hall as guests were shown around. In 1921, a second custodial building, Ward A, was added to house 160 girls. Both buildings had a separate sick room with one bed and a "strong room" with one cot, presumably used as an isolation room.

Two noncustodial buildings were added soon after. Ward L and Ward B were cross-shaped two-story buildings, each with porches large enough for beds and wheelchairs to be rolled outside, giving patients the benefit of outdoor air. Because the dorms were built on sloping elevations, the main entrance at the rear was two stories up even though the entrance led to the ground floor. Ramps were added to the raised staircases that made for easy access in and out of the dorms. While the basement of the custodial buildings had space for a number of trade shops, such as shoemaking or carpentry, the basements of these smaller wards instead held kitchens and dining areas for the residents. (Above, courtesy of Museum of disABILITY History.)

Wrentham State School continued to serve as the parent institution for Belchertown until construction was well underway on the main campus. When it was time for the Wrentham trustees to step back, the inaugural Belchertown State School Board of Trustees was chosen, and the first appropriations made independent of Wrentham were granted on June 1, 1922. The funds were authorized for the construction of a permanent administration building at the front of the campus, a schoolhouse with a gymnasium, two more dorms, two more employee cottages, and a permanent residence for the superintendent. The *Sentinel* was equally impressed by the school on its opening and remarked that, though it may have seemed in early days that the building of the school was little more than an economic chess move, meant to simply spend the state's money, it was immediately clear "when one has talked with those who are in charge of the institution and has gone into the rooms which the boys and girls will occupy, the human element displaces any commercial attitude."

The *Belchertown Sentinel* also remarked that Massachusetts "has more of these institutions . . . than many other states," three public and one private. This was not, it was noted, because there happened to be more feebleminded in the state, but because Massachusetts had become a leader

in the care and education of these students as evidenced by the success of the previous two schools in returning a good number of its students to their homes. The town already felt a growing sense of dignity in and friendship with the state school as it cemented its place in the landscape.

The request for a proper administration building was made by the trustees in the first annual report issued at the close of 1922. It was deemed inconvenient for visitors to have to navigate to the back of the campus to find the administrative offices that were located in the same building as the bakery and main kitchen. The trustees also complained that student records were accumulating faster than they could file them, and they did not have fireproof storage vaults for the files. This request was made a number of times before the legislature finally granted the funds for the new, modern Administration Building, which was completed in 1926. It, like the dorms, was an exact replica of the Administration Building at the Wrentham School. (Both, courtesy of Belchertown Historical Association.)

When the state school opened in 1922, there was no designated area for classrooms. Instead, a portion of the laundry facility was converted into a temporary school and assembly hall. Concerned that the teachers were not able to do their best work in such crowded conditions, the trustees requested a dedicated schoolhouse and gymnasium in the annual report at the close of 1925. The building was completed in 1928, becoming the central anchor of the cottage-style state school campus. Though the schoolhouse is listed as complete in the annual report for 1928, only four of the classrooms were open at that time, but it allowed the students to move from the laundry building into their permanent location.

The remaining portion of the building, including an auditorium that would seat 1,400 and the basement gymnasium, was not complete until 1932. The building also included a club room for employees, a canteen, and two bowling alleys. The schoolhouse would later host annual exhibitions of student work and farm products as well as weekly religious services, dances, and motion picture shows. Regular motion picture shows continued to be shown for years to come but were canceled in December 1946 because of misconduct—not on the part of the residents, but on the part of some of the boys from town.

The next most pressing need for the state school was a hospital, as the campus was too far away from any of the county hospitals. The appropriation for the hospital was allocated in 1929 and construction was nearly complete by the close of 1930. There were 60 beds on the second floor with open porches at the far end of the ward hallway as well as a suite of rooms for the live-in charge nurse. On the ground floor was a dental suite, an X-ray suite, a laboratory, a pharmacy, exam rooms, and waiting rooms. The hospital would serve all acutely ill patients and those recovering from surgeries, as well as sick employees and townspeople.

In the early years of the state school, the staff were required to live on campus. The first two employee cottages, appropriately named Cottages Nos. 1 and 2, were built in 1920 on the east side of campus closest to Ward A. White with green trim, the cottages were situated in groups of three along the outer edge of the campus, facing the wards so that each was in eyesight of the staff. The cottages would later be renovated to serve a number of purposes and would house a variety of programs, including transitional services for the residents going out into the community.

Blasting for tunnels began shortly after the first group of buildings was completed. Unlike state hospitals for the insane where tunnels were used to transport patients, the tunnels at the state school were meant to facilitate service to the heating and electrical systems. The extensive tunnel system was constructed largely by patients who assisted the construction crews. As more buildings were added, the tunnel system was expanded, and access points were added aboveground outside the employee cottages. The main tunnel access points were in the basements of the larger common spaces such as the schoolhouse, hospital, and nurseries. (Both, courtesy of Aubrey D. LaPolice Collection, University of Massachusetts Archives.)

In the early 1930s, two single-story nursery buildings were added at the front of the campus close to Route 202. Both buildings were built to care for the growing number of children under the age of seven being admitted to the state school. Each nursery had space for 50 children and a matron, as well as a sick room, serving room, and dining room. Nursery II, built in 1932, also had space reserved as a potential future classroom, but as of 1935, it was still vacant. In 1944, one of the resident's relatives donated a Victrola, along with a number of records, candy, and other small gifts, for the children to enjoy.

Industrial work, or handwork as it was called, was considered by the superintendent to be "wholesome, purposeful" work that provided the boys and girls at the state school with something of which to be proud. The industrial spaces were originally housed in the basements of Wards A and K but as the dorms grew more crowded, the need for living space forced the industrial departments out, and separate structures were built flanking the rear of the schoolhouse. The boys' industrial building was added on the west side of the schoolhouse in 1930. Built of brick that matched the ward buildings, the two-story rectangular building had space for larger, roomier shops where the boys repaired shoes, made brushes and brooms, and learned basic maintenance tasks.

For students whose academic education would be a much slower process, industrial work was immediate gratification that allowed them to celebrate more frequent milestones. Though they may have struggled academically, these students were able to showcase their talents at annual exhibitions. The girls' elaborate embroidery, woven rugs, and handmade clothing and linens were put on display. On the east side of the schoolhouse, the girls' industrial building was identical to the boys'. In addition to the shops, there was also space for the girls to exercise. Later, a beauty parlor was added in the basement, where it would remain until the 1960s.

MAY 33

The gymnasium was state of the art, with a balcony overlooking a basketball court and a full locker room with showers. Additional rooms were added to accommodate music classes as well as to provide smaller recreation spaces. A backstage area was constructed later as the recreation department's minstrel shows grew in size, necessitating more space for costumes and scenery. The schoolhouse served as the central gathering place well into the 1960s. Many of the committees on campus met in the employees' club room, and most presentations given by visitors were also held there. The auditorium was frequently loaned out for town activities, such as graduation exercises for the local high school and the celebration of the town's bicentennial.

One of the first and most elaborate holiday traditions established at the state school was the celebration of the Fourth of July. These events were orchestrated by the state school recreation department with assistance from the education department. The day began early with the raising of the flag followed by a parade. The parade floats and "ambulatory features" were constructed by the children under the supervision of the instructors in the girls' and boys' industrial departments. The floats represented subjects as up-to-date as The World of Tomorrow and as historical as John Paul Jones. Later activities included a field meet, baseball games, picnic lunch, and fireworks.

When the state school property was purchased, there were very few existing buildings that were sound enough to be used by the state school aside from the family farmhouses on Jackson Street that had already been converted into dorms. However, near the front entrance to the main campus, the state school property did absorb three family homes, including the Fairchild Cottage, pictured here, which was once used by the Fairchild family as a store but was converted into staff housing. The Riley Cottage was also used to house staff, and the third home, the Michel Cottage, became the assistant superintendent's residence.

VIEW FROM GYM 33 —MAY

By the mid-1920s, the state school had established itself firmly in the fabric of the town both as its largest employer and its largest supporter and contributor. Not only were superintendent George McPherson and his wife, Mabel, active in the church, but they had also forged deep and abiding friendships with the townspeople. The school's dentist and recreation director, Arthur Westwell, was a prominent member of the local American Legion and was elected president of the Belchertown Parent Teacher Association. The town celebrated the state school's victories and mourned its losses, its pride in the school already evident in every interaction and celebration.

Two

THE FARM

Once Belchertown was officially chosen as the location for the new state school, the first $50,000 was appropriated for the purchase of nearly 700 acres of land comprised of the Stacy, Witt, Michel, Howard, and Jepson farms. This early image shows one of the family farmhouses and the land that would become the state school.

Construction on the main campus moved slowly, but work on the farm was well under way. A group of boys from the Wrentham school moved into the abandoned Witt farmhouse and began to work the land. Mr. and Mrs. Hawes served as warden and matron of the farm and set out to welcome visitors from the town who wished to see the progress at the farm. In order to foster positive relations with the town, the local farmers were invited to come at any time to inspect the state school's agricultural operations and get ideas for their own farms. The townspeople were quite impressed with how well the crops were doing. There were 65 vegetable gardens growing 20 different types of vegetables along with a heated greenhouse for flowers and seedlings. Pictured here are the first patients in 1921. (Courtesy of Aubrey D. LaPolice Collection, University of Massachusetts Archives.)

At one time, the Commonwealth of Massachusetts owned more than 11,000 acres of working farmland within the state's institutional system. The farms supplied food for the institutions at a much lower cost than buying retail as well as furnished exercise and occupational training for the men who lived and worked on the farm. (Women were not permitted to live on the farm but joined the men in the summer to pick vegetables). When the farm was first organized, it was not only an economic decision, but like every program instituted in the state schools, farm work was also therapeutic, especially for the residents who were considered near normal intelligence.

The Belchertown State School farm had one of the largest dairy herds in the state and the highest milk production of all the institutional farms. Other livestock included chickens, pigs, and for a short time, turkeys. The head farmers of all the state institutions met regularly, and staff often moved between institutions as did crops, livestock, and equipment. Teams of residents were occasionally sent to sister farms, such as Myles Standish (later Paul A. Dever State School), to assist with more laborious tasks, like slaughtering pigs. When Northampton and Monson State Hospitals later closed their dairies, Belchertown received part of their herds in exchange for providing both hospitals with milk. (Below, author's collection.)

In addition to its formal ties to state institutional agricultural associations, the state school farm also established a number of connections with outside agricultural groups. Its most prominent memberships were in dairy clubs that frequently awarded the Belchertown State School herd their top prizes. The farm staff, along with groups of residents who cared for the cows, attended parades and fairs in surrounding communities where they often took center stage with their farm products and award-winning animals. Belchertown's farm quickly established connections with outside agricultural businesses and joined a number of agricultural associations, including the Eastern State Farmers Exchange, which would later merge with the Grange League Federation to become Agway and the Farm Bureau Association.

The town's history as a farming community played a large part in the legislature's decision to locate the state school there. More than 100 residents lived and worked on the farm, enjoying a great deal more independence than those living in the wards "up on the hill." The men in the farm dorms, also known as the farm colonies, were allowed to walk out in the fields and through the woods without supervision. They lived and ate their meals among the staff, having their own kitchen and their own cook. Those who worked the farm were affectionately known as "boys" regardless of their age or intelligence level.

Workhorses played a major part in the farming operations, especially when activities like logging and work in the swampy fields were best accomplished with literal horsepower. In the early years, they were also used to clear snow from the roads and sidewalks up on the main campus. Draft teams were far more economical than farm vehicles, and the horses were cared for by the tenants rather than by farm staff, freeing the staff up for other work. Workhorses were used for the entire time the farm was in operation. Later, the horses were used as part of a therapeutic equestrian program after the farm was officially shut down in the early 1970s.

Clearing Land.

Over time, there was a sharp increase of fruit and vegetables being produced by the farm, and a great matter of concern was now the storage of this produce, especially over the winter months. Storage space was so limited that the bumper crops of potatoes and apples collected in 1924 were left to rot, which was a great loss to the school. The school requested the funds to construct a proper root cellar, and it was completed in 1927. Funds were also requested for growing its small poultry plant and to construct a proper piggery. Eventually, a canning plant was also added so that residents could learn to can the leftover produce.

Eventually, it was clear that the farm's acreage desperately needed to be expanded. In 1926, the town gave the state the option to purchase the town poor farm on Jackson Street for $8,000. The farm included a two-story warden's department with an attached single-story ell that housed the lockup. When news of the sale broke, the townspeople assumed the state had brokered a secret deal with the school to purchase the farm for well under market value. Thanks to the superintendent, it was pointed out that, in fact, the poor farm was costing the town money, and the state was the only buyer willing to pay the town's asking price. The poor farm was acquired, and the tramp house converted into farm dormitories.

The farm was a jewel in the state school's crown and quickly became a source of pride for the town as well. The school's administration frequently made gifts, often in the form of produce or flowers from the farm or handicrafts made by the residents, for the community in order to show its appreciation. The farm grew enough produce and produced enough milk to supply both the school and the surrounding community. By the early 1930s, there were nearly 150 acres of land being farmed by the state school with the expectation that more would be cultivated as the number of mouths to feed increased.

Three

THE SCHOOL

The inaugural board of trustees was installed just in time to help choose the first superintendent. Dr. George E. McPherson, a native of Cambridge, Massachusetts, served as assistant superintendent at Foxboro State Hospital and Medfield State Hospital, and assistant executive officer at Boston Psychopathic. In 1921, he was promoted to assistant to Dr. George Kline, commissioner of mental diseases, who then appointed him superintendent of Belchertown State School in 1922.

McPherson's appointment was announced on March 15, 1922. He moved his wife, Mabel, their 11-year-old daughter Margaret, and 8-year-old son George Edwin Jr. to Belchertown. As the campus grew around him, McPherson hung a large map of the school on the wall in his office, a constant reminder of what he and his staff were building—a leading educational institution for the feebleminded. Applications for admission to the state school started strong and remained steady, showing no signs of slowing down. Children could be referred by the local public schools, identified through a school-based clinic, or referred through direct application by a parent or guardian. In the first year, 136 total applications were recorded, and there were 354 total admissions, 245 of which were transfers from both Wrentham and Waverley. A piece in the *Springfield Sunday Republican* described the opening of the state school as the "wheel . . . set in motion . . . [that] has completed its first revolution."

The press was invited to tour the campus, and the *Springfield Sunday Republican* was very impressed. Ward K, the first custodial building opened to residents, had a stunning view of the mountains on the horizon and the playgrounds outside. The rooms were comfortably furnished, and the entire building was warm and welcoming. There were even grand plans to outfit the basement of the building with pool tables for the boys to use when they returned from working on the farm; the younger boys who worked the farm were not permitted to live in the farm dorms and instead walked the dirt road back and forth each day.

Along with the two custodial buildings, two smaller plus-shaped brick wards were constructed in 1920 and 1921. Ward L and Ward B were both built to accommodate a total of 114 residents with room for a live-in matron. Without a central cafeteria space for taking meals, the wards had their own serving and dining rooms in the basement. There was not yet a separate infirmary, so each ward had a sick room of its own as well as a designated visiting area for family. On the second floor of Wards L and B, there was a well-stocked library, and a portable radio was purchased to be shared among the wards.

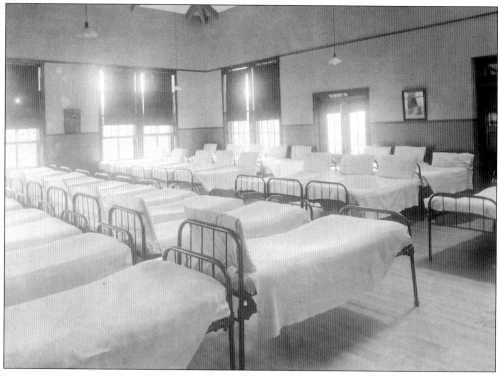

The day rooms of each dorm had soaring ceilings at 12 feet on the first floor and 15 feet on the second, with 10 windows each that reached nearly floor to ceiling. The second floor also had massive skylights to let in extra sun. In the basement, there was a large dining room with an attached serving room that had large sinks and a steam table. Off the serving room was a closet for dishes and flatware as well as a walk-in refrigerator. The food was not prepared in the dorms but brought to the wards from the main food service building.

Though the dorms had their own serving and dining rooms, a food service building handled the preparation and cooking of all the food on campus. Referred to as the canteen, the food service building also had a separate space for employees to take their meals during the day, as meals were included for staff. The canteen also sold the handiwork produced by the residents such as brooms, brushes, and linens, which provided enough profit to fund the purchase of radios for the wards as well as games and puzzles. Some of the funds also went to paying for special entertainment.

The storehouse at the rear of the campus supplied the canteen with most of its dry ingredients, and the bakery produced all of the baked goods served with meals. Extra dishes and serving pieces were also stored there alongside the food transport containers that were likely loaded into the back of trucks or carts and delivered to the canteen and, later, the dorms. The rail track ran right up to the loading dock of the storehouse, where train cars delivered supplies and equipment. There were also three walk-in freezers and space for dressing the meat that came up from the farm.

In order to address the steady influx of admissions in the first months of the school's operation, a social work department was established in March 1923 under the direction of Ruth Bolton from the Waverley school. She only remained at Belchertown until September 1, but in that time, she screened 104 referrals, 31 of which required further investigation. Forty-eight more cases referred from the community were investigated, only six of whom were admitted. Later, the social work department was responsible for placing residents in the community after "graduation" and maintaining the connection between the state school and the residents' homes.

D. M. D. Form A-5

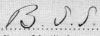

Name of Institution

PATIENT'S WARD CARD

N. B.—THIS card must always accompany every patient in all changes from ward to ward and attendants on ward are responsible for the same. The card must be returned to the office when the patient leaves the institution. When necessary, a new one can be obtained from the medical department.

Name .... *C* .... No. *1998*

Admitted *2 P.M* *Mar. 28* 193 *5* *B-3-24-32* Age *3 yrs* Height *2 ft*
         Hour   Date

Weight *26 lbs.*   Eyes *blue*   Hair *dk. brown*

Personal peculiarities and habits. Cautions as to escape, Self-injury, Violence, etc.

Microcephalic – speech defective

Cath.   *Dr. John T. Shea*
                                          Admitting Physician.

On admission, each patient's details were recorded by hand on a ward admission card that was coded with a number that correlated to the patient's main file. Each card recorded the patient's date and time of admission, age, date of birth, identifying characteristics, and general notes. The admitting nurse also noted what agency, if any, was financially responsible for furnishing the resident's clothing and personal items, and which physician approved the admission. The back side of the card recorded the patient's movement from ward to ward, dates of home visits or "parole," and eventual death, discharge, or transfer. (Both, author's collection.)

DATES OF TRANSFER.

N. B.—The **Ward Attendant** will in every case of transfer, sign his or her name **plainly** in the space opposite to the date thereby certifying that patient's clothing has been transferred to the ward named, and the Attendant receiving patient will **personally** see that such clothing is received at the same time with patient.

Date	Ward	Date	Ward
Mar. 28 193 *√* to Ward *Nurs.*		193 . to Ward	
June 6 193 . to Ward *D* *M.M.*		193 . to Ward	
May 9 193 . to Ward *B* *M.M.*		193 . to Ward	
MARCH 19 193 *46* to Ward *C (section) R.B.*		193 . to Ward	
MARCH 21 193 *46* to Ward *B* *R.B.*		193 . to Ward	
Nov. 4, 193 . to Ward *Q* *M.M.*		193 . to Ward	
APR. 28 193 *47* to Ward *MYLES STANDISH*		193 . to Ward	
	193 . to Ward		193 . to Ward
	193 . to Ward		193 . to Ward
	193 . to Ward		193 . to Ward

As the patient population grew, so too did the number of staff employed by the state school. This steady growth required the addition of five more employee cottages in the years between 1927 and 1930. A total of nine employee cottages were constructed at a cost of $27,500 each. The cottages were built for 22 employees each, mainly dormitory staff, and were fully furnished with private bedrooms, kitchenettes, and fireplaces in the common room. The cottages were comfortable, and room and board were included in the very generous employee benefits package. As well, all items such as food, furnishings, and linens were supplied by the school. Belchertown State School quickly became the town's largest employer, often employing multiple generations of local families. The staff hosted cookouts and other social events in the cottages, creating a family atmosphere both among themselves as well as for the residents.

"THE WEDDING OF THE PAINTED DOLL" B.S.S. 108

In 1924, Viola Cameron was hired as head teacher but was quickly replaced by Lucile Deatherage. McPherson made it a point to mention in the annual report that he was "able to secure the services of a competent head teacher so that the courses of study have been greatly improved," wryly implying that Cameron was not competent. Deatherage was to oversee the creation of a new curriculum, and by 1925, the school had added a kindergarten and six grades of grammar school. Despite the less than ideal space in the laundry building, the staff used it to its fullest potential for both education and entertainment. Pictured above is a 1929 minstrel show. The 1927 photograph below shows "story-telling hour" in the classroom.

Story-Telling Hour.

Dr. McPherson was immensely proud of the farm and its products and wanted to create an opportunity for the staff and residents to showcase the farm's abundant crops as well as examples of the extensive canning done by the residents. McPherson was also an avid gardener and enjoyed displaying the bounty of the school's flower gardens and greenhouses. He kept flats of flowers next to his garage to give as gifts and ate fresh fruit from the school's orchards. Artfully arranged fruits, vegetables, and flowers took center stage at the exhibitions, and the townspeople were duly impressed. Many of the farm's products were offered for sale both on campus and around town.

The first annual exhibition debuted in 1926 and an open invitation was printed in the *Belchertown Sentinel*. There were samples of crocheted rugs, intricate embroidery, and knitted sweaters and socks (some created by a blind student). All the materials on display were pieces made to be used at the school by both the children and the staff. A makeshift bedroom was set up to showcase the linens that were produced on the campus, as well as to show visitors what a child's room in the dorms might look like. The room was decorated with strings of glass and paper beads and visitors were welcomed in to look around. Each exhibit was supervised by the teachers and vocational directors from each department, and visitors were escorted by the children.

Holiday celebrations at the state school were taken very seriously by both staff and residents, particularly the recreation department, which staged elaborate minstrel shows. The Christmas shows were the most creative and best attended. The personnel from the recreation department assisted the school department in the preparations and maintained a sizable costume department with hundreds of costumes, many of which were made by the residents. During the winter months, these stage productions averaged about once a month, and occasionally, the residents tackled difficult plays, like a scaled-down version of Charles Dickens's *A Christmas Carol*. Participation in the shows was based on good behavior and a commitment to regular rehearsals.

For the holidays, gifts and donations were sent by numerous businesses, child aid societies, and wealthy local families to ensure that all residents received gifts and candy. As seen in these images, Christmas trees were also donated for the wards. Forbes & Wallace, Springfield's largest department store at the time, donated toys and packages while others donated ornaments, decorations, and lights. Holiday religious services were also provided, and formal dinners followed on the wards. After dinner, movies were shown on the wards, and gifts were distributed. The trees lining the campus roads were lit, and all the wards, including the farm colonies, were visited by Santa Claus.

CHRISTMASTYDE

at

BELCHERTOWN STATE SCHOOL
Belchertown, Massachusetts.

1927

MAY your Christmas be rich
with generosity to those who need
you, and your New Year big
with success and achievement.

The residents printed the tickets and programs for the holiday events and minstrel shows. In 1939, the education department assisted the residents in performing a shortened version of Charles Dickens's *A Christmas Carol.* They also put on a living manger scene along with a pageant reenacting the first Christmas.

Religious services were conducted each Sunday in the auditorium for both Catholics and Protestants. Special holiday services as well as burial services were also conducted when "desirable or necessary," according to the superintendent's annual report, presumably when a resident's family requested those services. The school choir, made up solely of residents, sang at all services and performed special music at Easter and Christmas. The state school also provided regular weekly religious education. In 1935, the religious services department expanded to offer services for the Jewish patients, which were conducted once each quarter. First Communion and Confirmation services were also conducted as part of the religious education program. Those services were generally presided over by local religious dignitaries. The town was welcome at weekly services, and the residents often attended services at the town churches. Many of the staff, including the administrative staff, were active members of the local parishes.

Throughout the year, but especially during the winter months, the school put on a number of indoor activities, such as dances and costume parties. Moving pictures were shown weekly, with additional pictures on holidays, as Arthur Westwell, the recreational director, was a licensed projectionist. Dances and ward parties were held bimonthly, and participation in recreational activities was used as a reward for good behavior. Town events and celebrations were also held in the auditorium. This image is likely from the annual Snowflake Ball hosted by the state school. Musical entertainment was provided by the residents and, occasionally, by outside volunteers. The residents were also responsible for decorating the auditorium and were encouraged to dress up for the events. It was one of the few times that male and female residents were allowed to socialize, and the staff capitalized on these opportunities to teach appropriate social skills.

In November 1944, Boy Scout Troop No. 509 was organized at the state school under the direction of John P. O'Connor, who was previously the scoutmaster of Troop No. 24 at the Hospital Cottages for Children at Baldwinville (now demolished). Thirty-two boys joined the troop and worked toward the same badges as the other troops in the area. The Scouts also attended special events and served as honor guard at both school and town events. Eventually, the Scouting program was expanded to include the girls as well, some of whom were also members of the school's precision drill and dance team.

From the time of its inception, the state school not only hosted its own holiday parades but also participated in the town celebrations. The school built its own floats using the farm vehicles, and the Scouts, along with the precision dancers, marched in the parades, the route winding through the state school campus. The Belchertown State School's fire chief and fire engine rode in the parade, as well as the school administrators, some of whom also held town offices.

In the warmer months, the state school provided as many outdoor activities as possible, like competitive team sports such as baseball and football, which taught important social skills. The school also hosted picnics, cookouts, and hiking parties. Each ward participated in monthly hot dog roasts and birthday celebrations. Later, the state school children participated in town sports as well, traveling for both basketball and baseball games. The scores of the various games played by the state school residents were enthusiastically recorded in the superintendent's annual reports.

On September 11, 1946, the school began a fundraising campaign to purchase a merry-go-round for the school. The children had ridden the carousel at the Belchertown Fair, and seeing how much they enjoyed it, families and employees supported the effort to get them their own. The first donation was made by one of the school's trustees, William Hyde of Ware. In 1948, the school acquired a Stein and Goldstein carousel for the residents, and it was officially dedicated on October 17. There was a parade to follow the dedication ceremony, and the children were given rides on the carousel.

Though there is no mention of it in the annual reports, the school also had its own miniature golf course at one time, seen here with the superintendent's cottage in the background. This course appears to have stretched across the front lawn of the state school where Route 202 now cuts through the original campus. Throughout the years, the school's recreation fund remained robust, accepting donations from numerous businesses, civic groups, and the employees themselves. This money funded a great deal of entertainment on the campus well into the early 1970s and also provided for trips to the Eastern States Exposition and Mountain Park in Holyoke.

FANCY-STITCHERS

The students' time was split evenly between schoolwork and vocational work; all residents would attend school for a half day and then spend the remainder of the day at their workstations. This was done in an effort to produce well-rounded graduates who could both read and produce quality handiwork. Dr. McPherson and Dr. Westwell gave a number of presentations about the benefits of hands-on work and regular recreation for state school residents. Industrial work provided the boys and girls with something of which to be proud. The school's consistent commitment to this balanced education earned them representation in the American Association for the Study of the Feeble-Minded, of which Dr. McPherson was elected president.

GIRLS EXERCISE CLASS
1929

Even in the winter months, regular outdoor activity was still encouraged. The children ice-skated on a homemade rink outside the storehouse at the rear of the campus and played in the snow. The draft horses were used not only for plowing the campus but also for giving sleigh rides through the fields. Indoor activities shifted to entertainment that was often provided by outside organizations. The friars from St. Hyacinth's Seminary in Granby (now MacDuffie School) visited Belchertown twice a week in the early 1960s, providing entertainment on the wards as well as hosting groups of residents at the seminary for concerts and shows.

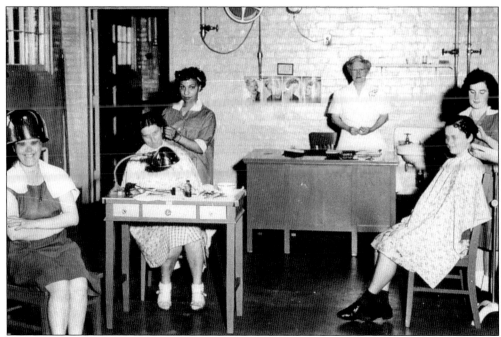

Along with providing ample entertainment, the school also endeavored to be self-contained and self-sufficient by providing resources such as an onsite beauty parlor and a barbershop. There the residents could not only get a haircut or shave from a staff member, but they could also learn how to style hair, apply makeup, and practice basic hygiene skills. The beauty parlor was in the girls' industrial building where the girls later learned how to color their hair or give a perm. The barbershop was on the ground floor of the boys' industrial building where it remained until the school's closure. Staff were also able to use the services of the beauty parlor and barbershop.

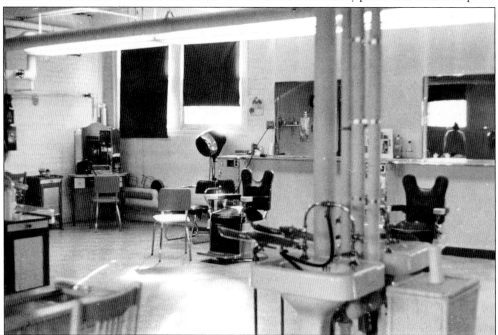

As part of its bid to be self-sufficient, the state school already had its own water source and sewage system and had established a campus-wide telephone switchboard system that was connected to the town's. In the early 1940s, it established its own fire department. The first fire truck was commissioned in early 1943. By 1944, the truck was completed just in time to make its maiden run on May 6 at 12:30 p.m. when a three-alarm fire broke out behind Webster's filling station. A group of state school staff and resident boys assisted in fighting the fire that spread through 75 acres of woods. (Both, courtesy of Stone House Museum.)

Though many residents were able to return home, some lived out their lives at the state school. A cemetery was established in 1925 and was neatly landscaped with bushes and flowers. Every Memorial Day, patients would walk over and lay flowers on the graves that were marked only by the patient's number chiseled into a rectangular stone. Taken on Memorial Day 1951, the image above shows flowers on the graves at the state school cemetery in a pine grove on the opposite side of Route 202. Relatives of deceased patients often brought flowers on Memorial Day as well.

Four

CHANGING TIMES

By the early 1940s, "Dr. Mac," as he was now known, was no longer able to serve as superintendent. The *Sentinel* announced the arrival of Dr. Henry A. Tadgell on July 11, 1943, and he took over the superintendency on July 15 when McPherson officially vacated the position. McPherson remained active on the campus until his death.

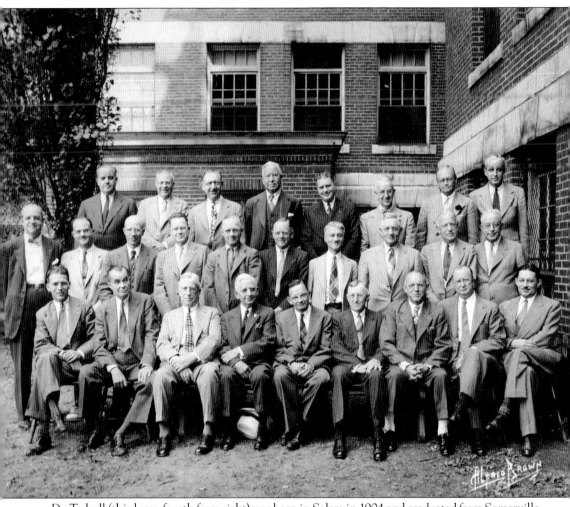

Dr. Tadgell (third row, fourth from right) was born in Salem in 1904 and graduated from Somerville High School in 1922. He went on to study medicine at Tufts College (now Tufts University) and trained at Wrentham State School before coming to Belchertown with a wealth of knowledge and experience in "mental cases." Tadgell and his wife, Esther, moved into the superintendent's house with their son Henry Jr., and the new superintendent was immediately tasked with keeping up the standards set by McPherson while World War II severely depleted his staff and his resources. Already, McPherson had apologetically announced to the town that for the duration of the war there would be fewer moving pictures and pageants; there would also be no more farm stands and livestock shows as much of the farm's output would go to supporting the war effort.

Taking on the superintendency in the midst of a world war meant working with a severely reduced staff and a tighter budget with no new appropriations on the horizon. It may have been assumed that campus activities would be completely suspended during wartime, or perhaps, visitors might not be welcome quite as often, but Tadgell was hesitant to put a stop to entertainment, especially so close to summer. He did his level best to run things exactly the way McPherson had but it seemed he had large shoes to fill and was not quite as highly regarded as McPherson, who had guided the state school through the Depression when jobs were especially hard to come by. McPherson was credited with keeping many families in town afloat and providing the town with plenty of meat and produce, which were in short supply as well. (Courtesy of Stone House Museum.)

The Fourth of July was right around the corner, and though McPherson had previously announced a cutback on entertainment, Tadgell saw no reason to cancel the celebrations. The activities would have to be scaled back a bit as there was not enough staff to assemble multiple floats and the farm vehicles were needed in the fields at all times, but there were still a few carts and tractors that could be pressed into service for the parade. Despite the limitations, the parade was a success, and a picnic lunch followed. The residents then gathered for a baseball game and a vaudeville show performed in the auditorium. In spite of the rational and thoughtful way that McPherson had announced the cutbacks, the residents of Belchertown were nonetheless affronted by the sudden distance between them and the school. Once Tadgell assumed the superintendency, the town inadvertently blamed him for the separation. (Courtesy of Stone House Museum.)

Tadgell also set out to keep the status quo when it came to both facilities' management and community outreach. He often gave lectures on the history of state institutions, as Massachusetts was one of the few states that took an active role in caring for the disabled rather than leaving it to families or to private institutions. On average, according to statistics at the time, one in every 22 individuals would likely spend time in an institution at some point in their lives, and state schools played a vital role in caring for them. The 1945 Annual Report of the Trustees noted that a number of visiting committees reported that the state school was giving "every attention to the health and welfare of the children." Pictured above are trustees James Harrop, Edwin Gilbert, Eugene O'Neil, Bertram Moody, William Hyde, Elizabeth Nash, and Margaret Torrey.

Division of Statistics, Massachusetts State Department of Mental Diseases

Belchertown STATE SCHOOL

Located at Belchertown, Mass.

TABLE 17. Clinical Classification of Cases in Residence on ~~September~~ June 30, 19. 45 , by Mental Status and Sex

Clinical Groups	Total			Idiot			Imbecile			Moron			Not Mentally Defective		
	M.	F.	T.	M.	F.	T.	M.	F.	T.	M.	F.	T.	M.	F.	T.
Familial	203	391	594	11	81	85	90	155	229	91	222	313	2	5	7
Mongolism	51	33	84	20	11	31	30	22	52	1	-	1			
With developmental cranial anomalies	17	11	28	9	3	12	6	6	12	2	2	4			
With congenital cerebral spastic infantile paralyses	20	17	37	9	8	17	10	8	18	1	1	2			
Post-infectional	30	34	64	8	5	13	14	15	29	7	13	20	1	1	2
Post-traumatic - natal	8	7	15	3	3	6	2	3	5	2	-	2	1	1	2
Post-traumatic - post-natal	2	-	2	1	-	1	1	-	1						
With epilepsy - symptomatic	1	6	7	-	1	1	1	3	4	-	2	2			
With epilepsy - idiopathic	12	8	20	8	4	12	2	4	6	2	-	2			
With endocrine disorder	3	1	4				1	1	2	2	-	2			
With familial amaurosis	-	2	2	-	2	2									
With tuberous sclerosis															
With other organic nervous disease	3	3	6	1	1	2	-	1	1	2	1	3			
Undifferentiated	196	232	428	52	46	98	80	81	161	61	101	162	3	4	7
Other forms	3	13	16	-	2	2	-	7	7	3	4	7			
Psychotic (not mentally defective)*															
Total	549	748	1297	125	107	232	243	284	527	174	346	520	7	11	18

*Placement of these cases in the mental status groups demonstrates the degree of deterioration due to the psychosis.

In order to provide the residents with an education targeted to their ability level, the "children" were classified by mental status, which was determined by a battery of tests given on admission. The resident doctors had examination rooms in the basement of the Administration Building where they asked general questions about the child's background and tested their basic knowledge. They also administered the Stanford Binet IQ test to arrive at a general estimation of the child's intelligence level. From that, the doctors assigned the children a mental age and entered it into their chart along with their "disability." This information was then collected at the end of each fiscal year and tracked in the superintendent's report, as seen in this chart that was included with the 1945 Annual Report of the Trustees. While these results were used to group the children for classes, the expectation was that they would be regularly retested and that their intelligence level would increase.

Even with a solid foundation of work, education, and entertainment, some of the residents still engaged in destructive activities from time to time. In August 1943, just two months into Dr. Tadgell's tenure, two farm boys placed railroad ties on the tracks behind the school with the intention of causing a wreck. The superintendent's report for that year notes that the obstruction was removed and no damage done. The boys were subsequently arrested and transferred to Bridgewater after admitting they wished to see the train "turn over and catch fire." Here is an early image of the track as a steam engine approaches through the snow. Within the first year of operation, the state school was granted permission to transfer the "defective delinquent" boys to Bridgewater, which was reported to have a "salutary effect." However, transfer was only allowed for boys aged 7 to 25. The trustees hoped in their annual report that provision would be extended to girls as well.

Though the general public was not aware of the issues Tadgell combated internally, they nonetheless had noticed the distinct difference between Tadgell's and McPherson's leadership styles. Despite Tadgell's best efforts, he seemed unable to forge the same connections with the town that McPherson had, putting a visible strain on the school's relationship with the townspeople. The change in atmosphere was also felt by many of the residents' families, who began to question the conditions at the school as well as the efficacy of the education programs. Some of the difficulties could certainly be attributed to the war, but most of it came down to Tadgell's inability to fill McPherson's shoes as the "father" of Belchertown State School. It might easily be assumed that Tadgell's role as superintendent was one that was accepted as necessary, but not necessarily embraced the way McPherson was. (Courtesy of National Register of Historic Places.)

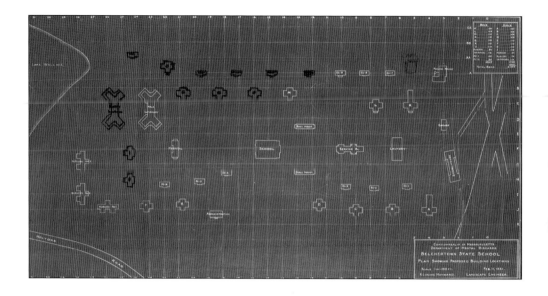

Tadgell may not have felt a kinship with the town, but he believed firmly in the future of the state school. In October 1943, Tadgell attended a meeting of superintendents at Boston's Hotel Kenmore where he proposed a number of postwar construction projects, including four more employee cottages, a contagious diseases hospital, two more boys' dorms, one more girls' dorm, two more nurseries, and a clinical research center. In the end, the only building that would be funded in the early 1940s was an infirmary. Though funds were released for the design and construction, it was not officially opened until 1952.

The close of 1943 and much of 1944 passed uneventfully until September 14, 1944, when an alert went out at 6:00 in the evening warning of an impending hurricane. The school partnered with the town immediately to prepare for the storm, connecting the town's pumping station to the state school's electrical system just in case the town's failed. The state school also assembled repair crews that remained standing by throughout the storm. Tadgell remained in constant contact with Northampton and Monson State Hospitals as well as sending hourly reports to the Department of Mental Health in Boston. Damage was, in the end, minimal with minor flooding in some of the employee cottages as well as some of the dorms, downed trees, and damage to the phone and power lines, which were all repaired quickly. In this image, crews, likely comprised of both staff and residents, clear downed trees away from the canteen.

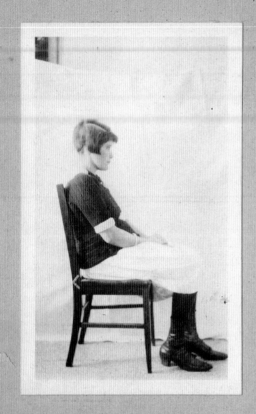

1925
Hydrocephalus.

C.A. $7\frac{2}{12}$
M.A. $6\frac{1}{12}$
I.Q. .07

The school recovered quickly from the storm and, on October 21, hosted the Regional Meeting of the American Association on Mental Deficiency held in the employees' club room. A lecture was given by Dr. Clemens E. Benda, clinical director of Wrentham State School, on "hydrocephaly," an accumulation of cerebrospinal fluid in the brain, which causes pressure inside the skull, resulting in cognitive delays and physical impairments. Hydrocephalus, as it is now called, can be treated by implanting a shunt that drains the excess fluid from the enlarged cranium. There was also a presentation on "Parent Education in a Child Guidance Program" by Olive Cooper, director of the Child Guidance Clinic, and on "The Hapsburg Lip: Its Origin and Spread Through European Royalty" by the state school's own junior industrial director Ethel Horsefield.

The lull in bad weather was short lived, and the winter of 1944 brought a great deal more snow than usual with most areas in Massachusetts reaching record snowfall totals. Frequent snowstorms in January 1945 caused a great deal of extra work for both the main campus and the farm group, but the school managed to reopen roads as quickly as possible both during and after each storm. Though they had purchased motorized snow clearing equipment, the school continued to use the draft horses to assist in clearing the sidewalks and much of the farm colony. They also loaned out their caterpillar snowplow as well as a group of residents to help clear the snow after the town's bulldozer broke down. As a reward for helping clear the snow, the residents were taken to Mountain Park that summer.

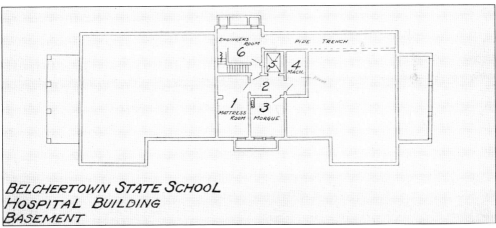

BELCHERTOWN STATE SCHOOL
HOSPITAL BUILDING
BASEMENT

Though capital projects were not yet being approved, the state school continued to implement smaller changes and advancements. Regular repairs were made to the buildings, and the maintenance department kept up with painting the wards and refreshing the furniture. The radiators and motion picture booth were also painted, and new woodwork was installed in the Administration Building. The head farmer's cottage was renovated and redecorated, as was the chief engineer's. In April 1945, a new mortuary unit was installed in the hospital's morgue. The unit had two drawers or trays connected to an electric refrigeration unit. However, the compressor and switchboard were not installed until the following year. The unit was switched on July 26, 1946. Also important that year was a reclassification of all employees and their salaries, which was sent off to Boston. It would later lead to changes in how vacancies were filled and how employees were compensated.

World War II had, so far, become the defining event of Tadgell's time at Belchertown until August 15, 1945, when the Japanese surrender to the Allies was reported. Tadgell's joy at the impending end of the war was evident in his report of that month, which was included in the annual report at the close of the fiscal year. Following the announcement, all employees were asked to remain on the clock and in their positions until the next day so that Tadgell could make arrangements to celebrate. A parade was held the next day, and there was an air of relief and joy on the state school campus. The next year, a "welcome home" parade was held in place of the regular Fourth of July parade to celebrate those returning from service. (Both, courtesy of Stone House Museum.)

Dr. McPherson remained active on the campus until his death on December 1, 1945. When the new infirmary finally opened in 1952, it was named in his honor, and a portrait of "Dr. Mac" was hung in the entryway. McPherson's death was eulogized more than once in the *Sentinel* but most eloquently in Belding Jackson's column, "The Steeple Soliloquizes." Under the pseudonym of "Bob Jackson," Belding penned his steeple column, which was written from the perspective of the Congregational church's steeple looking down on the town's activities. Jackson and McPherson had bonded over a mutual love of gardening and tennis.

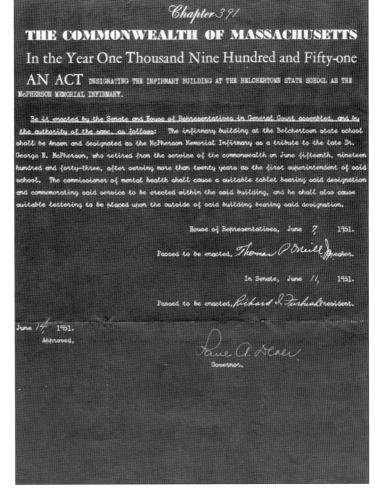

The McPherson Infirmary was built to house 224 boys and girls with severe physical disabilities as well as developmental delays. It was constructed in a double-Y shape, which created an elongated X shape from the air, a layout that was pioneered at Metropolitan State Hospital in 1934 and became a prominent style for medical buildings. It was two stories and built of the same brick as the rest of the campus. The infirmary was state of the art for its time and marked a shift in architecture from form to function with less attention paid to the building's appearance and more to its purpose. Two years after the completion of the infirmary, the state school's hospital, which was right next door, was fully approved by the American College of Surgeons. With these two specialized medical buildings, McPherson's legacy of high-quality treatment and top-tier education was more fully realized.

Come June 1946, Dr. Arthur Westwell and the recreation department helped the residents to put on the first full-scale summer minstrel show since the end of the war. The show was recorded on June 19 by Cora DeRose, director of the WHYN radio station and wife of Charles DeRose, publisher of the *Daily Hampshire Gazette* and president of the Tri-County Fair, which the state school residents attended each year for free. Motion picture recordings were also made of that month's show in hopes that reels with sound would be created and shown at the other state institutions. (Below, courtesy of Stone House Museum.)

Aside from participating in the minstrel shows, many of the residents also belonged to the Boy and Girl Scout troops. Thanks to a generous land donation from Guy C. Allen, the Scouts established a camp on the banks of the Swift River where they erected one cottage and a storage cabin in August 1946, both buildings constructed from wood donated by Mr. Pratt, a Belchertown farmer. The residents then went in groups of 25 to enjoy Scouting activities as a reward for good behavior. The camp grew over time thanks to canteen funds.

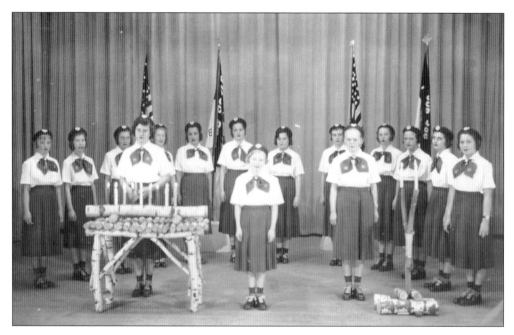

The general health of the institution was typically recorded as being relatively good, but given the close quarters in which the residents were living, an outbreak of tuberculosis (TB) seemed inevitable. In the late 19th century, TB killed one out of every seven people living in the United States and Europe. Also known as consumption, tuberculosis was once thought to be hereditary but was discovered to instead be highly contagious, with the tuberculosis bacteria thriving in close quarters where hygiene was lacking. In response to the TB epidemic of the 1940s, mass X-rays were conducted beginning January 21, 1947, to check for infection. That year, a few of the infected patients were sent to the Westfield State Sanatorium (pictured) in nearby Westfield where they later died as their lungs were destroyed by the bacteria. When the X-rays were completed, the equipment was sent on to Foxboro State Hospital. (Author's collection.)

In September 1948, the state school acquired a "twin coach" bus from the Eastern Massachusetts Street Railway, purchased through the Department of Mental Health. The bus could hold 30 and was used to transport residents to and from the carousel park, as well as to activities in town and at other institutions. The bus was said to be in "fairly good shape" and allowed a larger group of residents to attend the Eastern States Exposition, which they visited every year. That year, the bus was also used to transport First Communion candidates to St. Francis Church in Belchertown. Transportation was not always necessary for events off campus. When the residents attended the Three-County Fair at the invitation of Charles DeRose, transportation was provided free of charge by the Northampton Street Railway Company.

Major changes on the campus were made in 1949 beginning with the resignation of the dentist and recreation director, Arthur Westwell, who had accepted a post as superintendent at the Montana State Training School in Boulder. Shortly after his departure, the stone gates and wall at the entrance to the school were removed to make room for the new "highway" (Route 202) being built that would divide the superintendent's house and the Pine Grove Cemetery from the rest of the campus. That summer also saw the beginning of controversial fluorine trials at all three state schools. In the early 1940s, public health officials were unsure how safe fluoride would be when ingested. The state legislature suggested that fluoridation be studied at the state schools and secretly chose Wrentham and Belchertown as test subjects. The existence of these trials would not be acknowledged until 1994, when reports of radioactivity testing were also released. (Courtesy of Stone House Museum.)

Other changes, many on the bureaucratic level, began to make waves on the state school campus. The first of these affected the employees on a large scale as the state now required all employees to begin renting rooms, apartments, suites, or cottages, preferably off campus. In order to encourage this move, the state mandated that meals no longer be provided for free. Instead, meal tickets would be sold at 30¢ each. Food and supplies for the employees still living in the cottages on campus would have to be purchased elsewhere. Dr. Tadgell knew this would lead to a number of resignations, as would the strict 40-hour workweek being imposed down on the farm, and indeed, it did result in a great deal of turnover as room and board was initially one of the greatest employment benefits. The lack of flexibility on the farm meant that more staff would have to be hired in order to cover the hours that were cut to create the shortened workweek.

Dr. Tadgell's personal life also experienced a good deal of upheaval with the passing of his wife, Esther, on February 21, 1948, after an unexpected illness. The following year, on March 21, 1949, Tadgell married Lucy Bortkiewicz, who had been supervising the state school hospital unit since 1944. She had previously worked with Tadgell at Wrentham State School. A reception for the couple was held on March 23, and the two honeymooned in Maine. When they returned, they moved into a new home five miles away in Amherst, leaving the superintendent's house vacant. Later, the superintendent's cottage was converted into a temporary tuberculosis ward in order to separate those who were infected from the rest of the resident population. Also in 1948, a building survey was conducted, finding a total of 114 structures on the campus connected by 7,854 feet of tunnels.

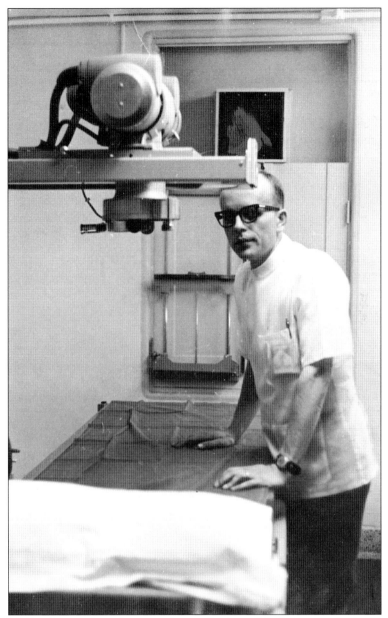

By the mid-1940s, the number of patients being discharged had decreased substantially while admissions remained steady, the patient census either remaining the same or increasing over the course of each fiscal year. At the same time, the number of qualified staff members filling professional positions at the state school had steadily decreased. A number of these key positions remained vacant including X-ray technician, assistant physician, and numerous licensed registered nurse positions. There remained a shortage of ward staff as well, especially on the female wards. The school was also facing unexpected funding shortages, maintenance issues, and rodent infestations. The position of dentist was technically empty, but the state had yet to officially announce the vacancy, so it could not be filled until Arthur Westwell was removed from the state school payroll. A temporary TB ward was established in the infirmary until 1956, when it was moved to the superintendent's house.

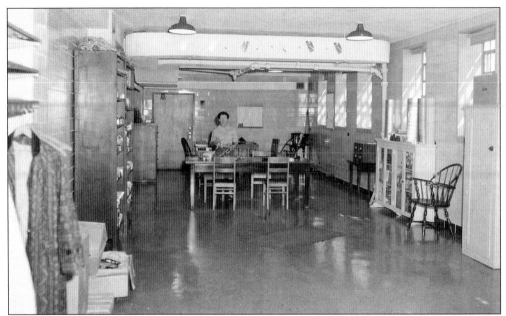

The overall funding shortages as well as concerns about the conditions at the state school led to the creation of a parents' group. Desperate to bring some creature comforts to the residents, the group began to sponsor birthday and holiday celebrations and maintained a fund for small repairs. On May 11, 1954, the group officially became the Belchertown State School Friends Association. At the same time, a robust volunteer program had begun, led by women from the Westover Air Force Base Officers' Wives Club. They provided entertainment for the nursery children every afternoon and brought gifts for the wards. In January 1958, Barbara Valliere was appointed supervisor of volunteer services, managing 51 volunteers putting in more than 334 hours since the program's inception only a month earlier.

Given the continued influx of admissions, Dr. Tadgell surmised that there would be a need for at least four more state schools in Massachusetts at a cost of $12 million. At Belchertown especially, admissions of children under the age of seven made it necessary to construct a third nursery. On February 17, 1960, ground was broken behind the hospital building. The nursery was built to house infants and the youngest of the children on campus in a sprawling, modern single-story building with a basement. The building had a jungle gym and well-stocked play spaces though the patient-to-staff ratio was rather high, meaning that often the children in the new building, later named for Superintendent Tadgell, often sat on the floors doing very little. In an effort to bring a bit of joy to Nursery I, the volunteers of the Westover Wives' Club painted the day rooms with flowers, sunshine, and butterflies, calling it "Fairyland."

The early 1960s ushered in a new era at the state school, and for the first time, the state was concerned for the future of the state school residents, especially those who had lived most of their lives in the state's care. Also, Dr. Tadgell was preparing to retire from the state school as of June 1960. He had already filed his paperwork, and a reception was given in his honor on June 22. By July 1, 1960, Dr. Lawrence Bowser was installed as assistant superintendent in preparation for Tadgell's departure, when he would take over as superintendent. Tadgell's retirement was made official on July 31, 1960, on which date Dr. Bowser assumed the superintendency of the state school. Dr. Tadgell passed away on December 3, 1963, and a memorial service was held in his honor in the auditorium on December 9.

Five

PURGATORY

Early in Bowser's tenure, it was clear that conditions at the state school had deteriorated substantially. Whether or not this turn of events could be laid solely at Bowser's feet has been hotly debated. Some argued that the circumstances leading to the school's decline had already been in place for much of Tadgell's time in office. Others firmly believed that Bowser's ineptitude was the turning point for the state school.

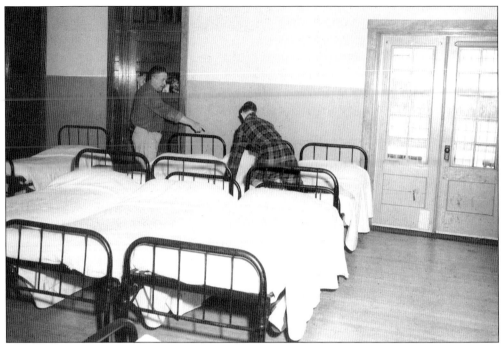

Staff turnover was the highest it had ever been, and education was no longer a priority at Belchertown. Instead, resident control and personal safety became of utmost importance. The doors to the buildings were locked as were the doors inside, forcing residents into communal spaces with no choice in how they spent their days. The wards were beginning to resemble prison dorms as opposed to living spaces. Televisions were secured in wire cages and furnishings were minimal, institutional, and uncomfortable. Restraints were being used regularly, resulting in an increased number of injuries, and creature comforts on the wards were few and far between.

Beginning in the 1960s, residents were stripped of their personal belongings on admittance. They were allowed to keep only what would fit on one or two shelves of the free-standing wardrobes on the wards, and personal hygiene products were in short supply. Inside the wards, the beds were stacked head to foot with a mere 12 inches of space between each row, forcing residents to climb over others to get into bed. There were no longer rugs on the floors or decorations on the walls, and heavy grates had been installed on all the windows. The dorms were dirty, damp, and dark.

As conditions continued to deteriorate, the presence of the Belchertown State School Friends was the only saving grace for the residents. Its influence led to a sharp increase in volunteerism and encouraged a greater deal of transparency in the reports that were being shared with the public, who were finally being made aware of the glaring deficiencies at the state school. Though there was still a recreation fund, it now fell to the volunteers to provide entertainment, personal items, and holiday celebrations rather than being provided by the school as in the past. By 1965, there were more than 800 volunteers on the state school campus.

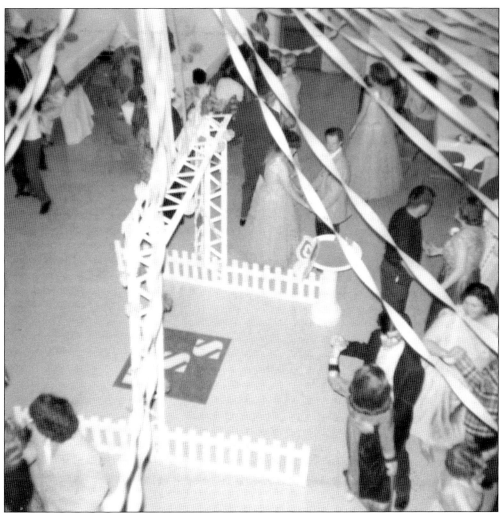

The Belchertown State School Friends worked to regularly host parties and monthly dances, like this one in the auditorium. The original parquet floor of the schoolhouse had been damaged, and in August 1968, a tile floor, with the Belchertown State School's initials at the center, replaced it. Music for the dances was often furnished by volunteers and from the Holyoke Musician's Union. They also hosted Halloween parties and Christmas celebrations on the wards where they delivered gifts and candy to the residents. The volunteers also went out into the community to educate the general public on the programs at the state school and to recruit more volunteers. They forged connections with the education and psychology programs at the local colleges, recruiting groups of volunteers in need of special education experience.

The growing number of volunteers on campus worked to institute a number of programs that would help break up the monotony of the residents' lives at the state school. They began with the birthday box, which provided individually chosen birthday gifts for each resident. Over several months, volunteers set up collection stations at Stop & Shop supermarkets in Springfield, Holyoke, and Northampton to gather books of trading stamps. In all, the volunteers collected 3,840,000 trading stamps, which they exchanged for a brand new 60-passenger bus that would be used for a variety of outings, much like the older bus that had been acquired in the 1940s. The bus, named the Birthday Bus as part of the birthday box program, was delivered in February 1963, and a ceremony was held both outside and inside the Administration Building.

While the Birthday Bus was the largest and most public volunteer success, many other programs on the state school campus were being undertaken. Most importantly, the volunteers were responsible for ensuring that the residents received Christmas gifts and regular birthday celebrations. The Women's Guild of the Congregational Church in Belchertown went so far as to sponsor a "substitute parent" program in which volunteers "adopted" a particular patient to visit, write to, and take home for dinners and holidays. Graduate students also spent a great deal of time helping to get patients out of the wards and onto the grounds, taking them for walks.

As on-campus entertainment diminished, the exquisite state school carousel fell into disrepair. It had not been adequately sheltered, and the harsh New England weather had taken its toll, leaving the carousel inoperable. The State School Friends stepped in and raised $20,000 to restore it. The horses were repainted, and their glass eyes and real horsehair tails were replaced. The carousel was moved closer to the wards, and a prefabricated metal building was erected to house it, but its new lease on life was short. The carousel was eventually closed completely and auctioned off by the State School Friends to help defray the costs of repairs elsewhere on the campus.

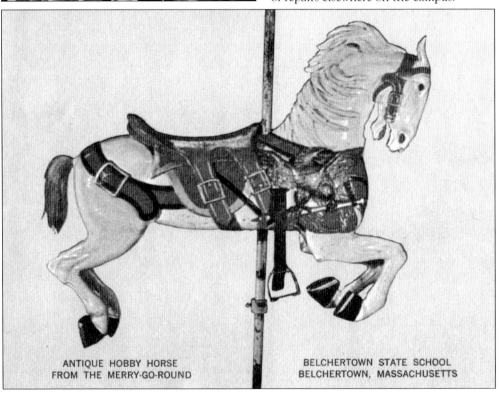

ANTIQUE HOBBY HORSE
FROM THE MERRY-GO-ROUND

BELCHERTOWN STATE SCHOOL
BELCHERTOWN, MASSACHUSETTS

While the focus of the state school shifted away from education, some of the previous vocational and industrial practices continued, especially use of the woodshop and the printing shop. Both provided a great deal of low-cost labor for the campus, producing items that were used regularly. The woodshop made everything from brushes and brooms to furniture and storage. They also did a great deal of repair work. Despite the decline in the quality of education, there were still dedicated classrooms and a small team of teachers still working to teach some of the residents to feed and dress themselves, while others learned the alphabet and how to spell their own names.

For 70 years, the state school was the largest employer in Belchertown. At its peak population, the state school employed nearly 1,500 people, more than one third of whom lived in town. Employment at the state school, similar to other state institutions, became a family affair, a generational commitment that created at least a shadow of the home-like atmosphere that once existed when the state school first opened. Despite the relatively high turnover of the late 1960s and 1970s, there was a core group of employees who had been there for a decade or more, many of whom would celebrate 25 years at the institution.

The state school department heads made numerous attempts to create stronger education programs. They planned for the creation of a practical nursing program in 1965 and made numerous visits to observe education programs at other state schools. Hoping to start a teacher training program for teachers that was specific to special education, the head of the school program even visited the University of Massachusetts, but there was little follow-through in implementing these potential changes. However, the home economics classes flourished, and industrial education remained steady, placing the focus squarely on vocational skills rather than education. The state also began the practice of filling professional positions with candidates who were not licensed to practice in the United States.

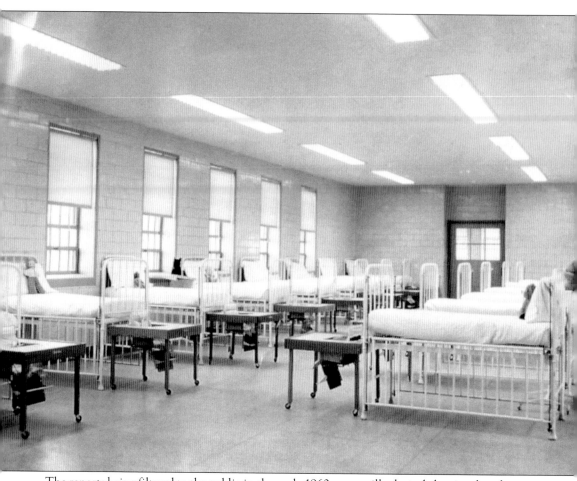

The reports being filtered to the public in the early 1960s were still relatively benign, but that was about to change abruptly. In 1965, a scathing exposé, complete with hidden camera photographs, was published by Fred Kaplan and Dr. Burton Blatt, who visited a number of state schools in New England with the intention of announcing to the public the degradation of these institutions. At the time, the "hell on earth" visited in the book went unnamed, but eventually the world learned

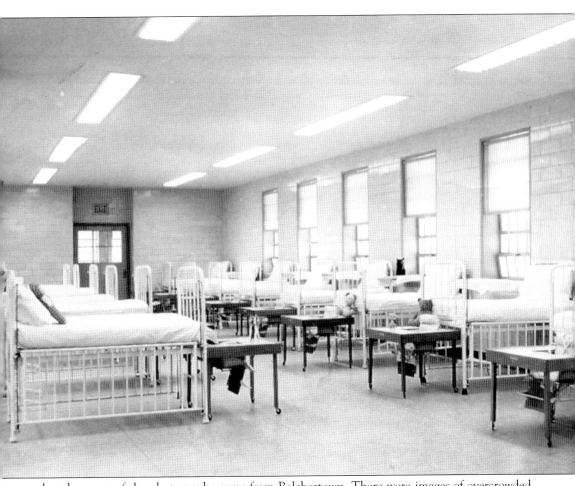

that the worst of the photographs came from Belchertown. There were images of overcrowded wards and children laying in their own filth. There were images of patients in restraints with atrophied limbs, curled in the fetal position. For many, it was the first glimpse inside the world of the institutionalized. (Courtesy of Stone House Museum.)

In 1969, William Fraenkel, assistant commissioner for mental retardation, spent 24 hours at Belchertown State School, all of which he found deplorable. His resulting report was published as part of the 1971 Joint Commission Report on the conditions at both Belchertown and Monson. As Robert Hornick suggests in his book, it is unclear whether or not the full report was shared with Superintendent Bowser, but Fraenkel certainly sent a memo with suggestions for a number of improvements on campus. A number of reforms were indeed instituted at the school, but none of them were sufficient or sustainable. Fraenkel revisited the school a month later to find that few of his suggestions had been implemented, and those that had were ones that made the least impact on the greater population. The Joint Commission determined that exactly four of Fraenkel's recommendations had been implemented.

Fraenkel had suggested regular weekly visits to each building, making building cleanups a priority in order to combat the pest problem, which by now was out of control. He also suggested the elimination of seclusion rooms and restraints, but as is evidenced by maintenance reports taken by the superintendent, the seclusion rooms were still being regularly maintained. Most importantly, Fraenkel suggested creating more opportunities for patients to get out and exercise while also making an effort to reevaluate and discharge patients who were able to get and keep gainful employment and community housing. Bowser had indeed achieved a major reduction in population between 1966 and 1970, but again that was due not just to regular discharges, but also to transfers to other institutions as well as a temporary freeze on admissions. He did however succeed in significantly improving the staff-to-resident ratio, bringing it to 1:2 by 1970.

In the March 15, 1970, edition of the *Springfield Union*, reporter James Shanks further described the conditions at Belchertown. He had been invited to tour the campus by M. Philip Wakstein, a regional administrator for the Department of Mental Health. Shanks was especially horrified by the custodial wards where 120 men lived in Ward K with no toilet seats and no partitions in the bathrooms. There were three attendants for those 120 residents, all of whom ate their food mixed indiscriminately in a metal bowl. Wakstein was quoted as saying, "The only difference between Belchertown and Auschwitz is the lack of gas chambers." It was decided that Ward K would be closed by Christmas while the women's ward would be closed by Labor Day 1971.

Construction on the new G Building for male patients began in May 1966. The new ward was overcrowded only weeks after its opening, yet for some reason, the school was regularly returning unused funds to the state, spending less on each patient than the other state schools in Massachusetts. To a large extent, and in some ways rightly so, the employees at the state school blamed Supt. Lawrence Bowser for the deteriorating conditions and petitioned the commissioner of the Department of Mental Health to fire him. The push to remove Bowser from the superintendency continued until he voluntarily resigned in March 1971.

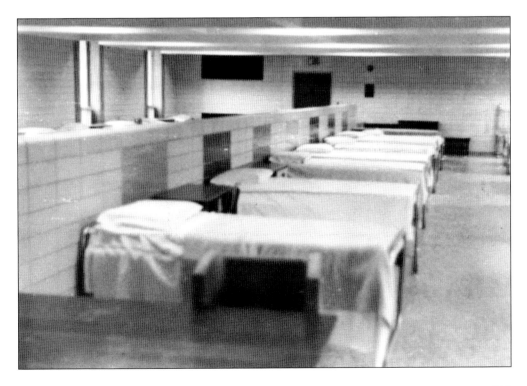

James Shanks's "Tragedy of Belchertown" series in the *Springfield Union*, which now ran weekly and had its own section in the paper, also documented the overcrowding in the nurseries as well as the McPherson Infirmary, which had become another "back ward" where the youngest residents spent most of their time unsupervised in large day rooms on cold floors. The rest spent their days in bed. The state school attempted to defend itself against Shanks's attack with "An Objective Review of Belchertown State School," which was anything but objective. The Department of Mental Health's response was to appoint a special commission to investigate both Belchertown and Monson over a one-year period. (Above, courtesy of National Register of Historic Places.)

By the mid-1960s, the superintendent's reports began listing "discharge by death" as an acceptable means of decreasing the patient population. Also, Dr. Bowser began regularly authorizing patient transfers from Belchertown to the many state hospitals for the insane in Massachusetts. In many cases, severely disabled patients were being shuffled onto the wards of equally overcrowded asylums with the severely mentally ill. Shanks's "Tragedy of Belchertown" remarked that "death was almost the only exit from the institution."

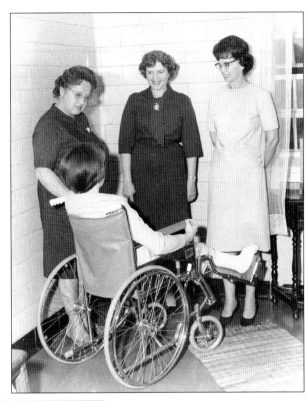

There were more than 75 vacancies on the staff while much of the important work on campus, including "speech improvement," occupational therapy, and physical therapy, was being done by volunteers. Even braces and wheelchairs were being purchased using donations raised by volunteers. Official physical therapy and speech and hearing departments were not established until 1966, when the school received a grant that would provide $98,395 annually to build these departments over three years.

In 1968, Dr. Benjamin Ricci, a member of the Belchertown State School Friends Association, was elected president. It had become clear that, though the association's initial intent was to simply better the lives of the residents through fundraising and volunteerism, providing creature comforts, and opportunities to socialize, the group was now developing a political agenda as well. It was falling to them and the other volunteers to take action and arrive at potential solutions to a number of the problems on campus that the administration seemed unable to resolve on its own. The association became instrumental in the fight to bring Belchertown into the 20th century.

Donald Vitkus (at right, and below, seated) was only six when he arrived at the state school in 1949. His IQ score was just 41, which classified him as a moron. He remained at Belchertown until 1960, enduring abuse and neglect at the hands of his caregivers. In 2005, he met former English teacher Ed Orzechowski (below, standing) at a book signing for Dr. Ben Ricci's book *Crimes Against Humanity: A Historical Perspective*. Vitkus was now a 66-year-old student at Holyoke Community College and had arranged Ricci's signing. He approached Orzechowski and explained that he was looking for someone to write about his time at Belchertown. *You'll Like It Here: The Story of Donald Vitkus, Belchertown Patient #3394* was published in 2016. Donald Vitkus passed away in 2018. (Both, courtesy of Ed Orzechowski.)

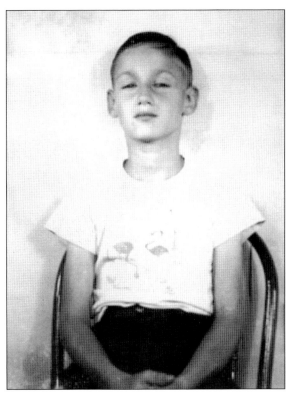

Ruth Sienkiewicz-Mercer was diagnosed with cerebral palsy when she was 13 months old after a bout of encephalitis. She was committed to Belchertown as a teenager when it became too much for her parents to care for her at home. She spent most of her time on a ward with schizophrenics, unable to communicate her needs. In the 1960s, after a severe break to Ruth's hip, one of the ward attendants realized Ruth could communicate with eye movements. Eventually, she was provided with a communication board, which allowed her to write her memoir, *I Raise My Eyes to Say Yes*, with the help of Steven Kaplan. The book was first published in 1989 and was the winner of the Christopher Award in 1990. Ruth married fellow resident Norman Mercer in 1980, and they lived together independently until her death in 1998. (Above, courtesy of Steven Kaplan.)

Jeromie Whalen, a technology teacher at Northampton High School, was completing his undergraduate degree when he chose Belchertown State School as the subject of his capstone project: an hour-long documentary on the history of the state school. The resulting film, *Purgatory: A Historical Analysis of the Belchertown State School*, won the national Hometown Award. The documentary, which he produced while completing his internship at Northampton Community Television, includes extensive interviews with Don LaBrecque and former patient Donald Vitkus as well as former assistant superintendent Bill Zimmer. Most recently, Whalen was also recognized with the 2019 Pioneer Valley Excellence in Teaching Award. The documentary is available to view online. (Both, courtesy of Jeromie Whalen.)

Don LaBrecque was a trainer in the Central West Region of the Department of Mental Retardation, which later became the Department of Developmental Services. An avid historian, he saved as much state school history as he could, amassing an incredible library of images that detailed the history of both Belchertown and Monson. He developed a handbook of sorts titled *A Historical Perspective on the Lives of People Labeled With an Intellectual Disability in Massachusetts*, which was printed by the Department of Developmental Services in 2002. He distributed the handbook to his training groups. It traced the history of state institutions for the feebleminded, giving an overview of the evolution of the care of the developmentally disabled. Don LaBrecque passed away in 2014 after nearly 34 years with the department.

ABOUT THE ORGANIZATION

The mission of the Belchertown State School Friends Association is to preserve the history of the state school and of the treatment of individuals with developmental disabilities. While the mission has evolved greatly since the original friends were founded in 1954, its aim is to continue the legacy of community engagement, education, and outreach. To find out more information and become a member, visit www.bssfriends.org.

DISCOVER THOUSANDS OF LOCAL HISTORY BOOKS
FEATURING MILLIONS OF VINTAGE IMAGES

Arcadia Publishing, the leading local history publisher in the United States, is committed to making history accessible and meaningful through publishing books that celebrate and preserve the heritage of America's people and places.

Find more books like this at
www.arcadiapublishing.com

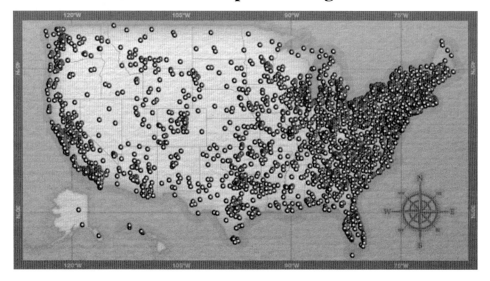

Search for your hometown history, your old stomping grounds, and even your favorite sports team.

Consistent with our mission to preserve history on a local level, this book was printed in South Carolina on American-made paper and manufactured entirely in the United States. Products carrying the accredited Forest Stewardship Council (FSC) label are printed on 100 percent FSC-certified paper.

MADE IN THE USA